Meditation

Simple Instructions On How To Meditate In Order To
Live A Happy Life Free From Stress

*(Scripts That Enable Instant Relaxation And Self-discovery
For Empowering Use)*

Darcy Rose

TABLE OF CONTENT

What Are The Benefits Of Meditation To Your Life? 1

Position For Meditative Pointing............................ 7

The Benefits That Meditation Can Have On The Body 22

How To Get Rid Of Stress Through Meditation 39

The Fundamentals Of Meditation: An Outline And Guide To Getting Started 43

A Brief Explanation Of Psychic Capabilities 59

The Importance Of Practicing Meditation For Five Minutes 66

Meditation While Assuming Various Positions 70

Why Should One Meditate According To Buddhist Principles? 74

Effective Advice On How To Meditate 78

What Does It Mean To Meditate With A Guide? 87

Advice On Establishing A Routine For Daily Meditation 96

The Dance Of Giving And Receiving That Occurs Between Children And Their Parents.............. 102

Techniques Of Meditation That Are Simple To Perform 108

Meditation For Kids, Both Beginners And Busy Kids' 111

The Importance Of Modesty In Meditation ... 117

The Brain Of An Active Elderly Person 129

The Beginnings Of A Meditation Practice 137

What You Need To Know Before Engaging In Imaginative Meditation 144

What Are The Benefits Of Meditation To Your Life?

To put it another way, meditation is a state of consciousness in which the mind is calm and unagitated. When the level of stress becomes intolerable, we all need assistance in finding a healthy way to deal with it. Some people depend on external stimuli to divert their attention away from their anxieties, while others find that meditation is the most effective way to still their racing thoughts. The practice of meditation may assist you in taking command of what is occurring in your head, which in turn enables you to better manage your emotions.

Numerous studies have shown the extraordinary positive effects that regular meditation may have on a person's life. Not only is it a method for getting in touch with oneself, but it also has the potential to be an energizing and uplifting experience. Here are a few particular ways that regular meditation practice may assist to enhance your life, in case you're still on the fence about whether or not it's something you should do.

Enhances one's capacity for attention and concentration

It is time to put your thoughts back in order if you notice that you are always allowing yourself to get sidetracked by the most insignificant of issues. Meditation may assist enhance attention and concentration, allowing you to more easily complete tasks at the precise moment they are required of you. Sometimes our minds get so preoccupied with everything going on around us that it becomes difficult for us to concentrate on a single topic. According to recent studies, multitasking isn't going to cut it anymore; thus, if you require higher brain capacity to perform just one thing at a time, then you need to strengthen your ability to focus and concentrate in order to accomplish this goal.

Fosters a greater sense of self-awareness

Meditation on a regular basis does more than merely cleanse the mind. Additionally, it assists you in developing a greater awareness of your sense of self. It has the potential to assist you in recognizing who you are at your very essence. Meditation can help you cleanse your mind and assist you in working over your shortcomings, regardless of what those shortcomings may be. Spending some time to get to know oneself better is perhaps the single most effective strategy for achieving a state in which you are at ease in your own skin.

Promotes more acceptance

Experts claim that if you want to achieve pleasure in your life, the single most important skill you can acquire is acceptance, and one of the best ways to develop acceptance is to practice the discipline of meditation. The practice of meditation may assist one in coming to terms with the realities of life. When you delve into your own psyche, you eventually come to the conclusion that some aspects of your life are beyond your ability to influence or change. You realize that there is no use in continuing to struggle, and you learn how to let go and just go with the flow. Once you have begun to accept yourself, it will be much simpler for you to accept others and the circumstances in which they find themselves. This process may take a lifetime.

Promotes the adoption of a healthy way of life

You no longer need to depend on crutches to give you the calm that you've been yearning for since meditation will offer you the center that you need. You'll acquire a taste for natural, fresh vegetables, which you'll want to eat more of rather than reaching for meals high in sugar and fat. When you're under pressure, you should also consider reducing the amount of alcohol you drink. This will serve you well. There are also some who have given up smoking because they no longer see the value in doing so. As soon as you begin to meditate, you'll have a strong desire to improve your health and become a better person overall.

Combats the visible effects of aging

According to a number of studies, the practice of meditation may have such a significant influence on the functioning of the brain that it can actually retard the aging process. People who meditate on a regular basis are shown to have a greater amount of gray matter, or brain cells, than those who do not. When a person has more gray matter, they are able to react better to stress, which gives them a higher chance of warding off any indications of aging that may appear.

Meditation is a strong tool that will help you get to a state that you want to be in It may not be the one stop answer to a better life, but it is one tool that will help you get there. You must not let the challenges of life to get you down. Spending as little as a few minutes every day meditating is all it takes to start reaping the advantages of this practice.

Position For Meditative Pointing

To successfully practice meditation according to the Tibetan Buddhist tradition, one makes use of the seven points of Vairocana. You may cultivate awareness, acceptance, and knowledge inside yourself via the practice of meditation by adopting the seven-point meditation posture, which is described in detail below.

The first step in posture is to sit down.

The very first and most fundamental step is to assume a seated position on the ground. If you are used to sitting on a chair, this may make you feel awkward or weird at first, but after giving it a few tries, you will eventually get used to the new routine and won't even notice the difference. To sit on the ground in a manner that is comfortable and conducive to productive meditation, you may experiment with a variety of various postures. You are free to choose the one that is most suitable for you.

As a novice, it is highly crucial to concentrate on the location of the meditation session before going on to choose a meditation position. The environment in which you meditate may have a significant impact on your ability to maintain concentration throughout the practice. If you are trying to meditate in a loud environment, you will most likely have a difficult time concentrating on the actual practice at hand, and you will discover that your concentration wanders off very often.

Additionally, the location in which you meditate has to be tidy, well-organized, and free of unnecessary distractions. Messy and chaotic surroundings may be a source of distraction in several ways. As soon as you take a seat in that location, you are very likely to concentrate on any object that is contributing to the clutter in the surrounding area, get uncomfortable because of the mess, or have a sense of being overwhelmed. Therefore, when you sit down to meditate, choose a location that is spotless, well-organized, serene, and free from everything that can cause you to get distracted.

It doesn't matter whether you meditate in a corner of your home, a whole room, a secluded area in your garden, or even in your vehicle; the important thing is to find a setting that allows you to relax and concentrate more easily. You should clean the area, and if it's okay with you, you may put anything there that calms your mind and helps you connect with the spiritual aspect of yourself. It might be a little statue of the Buddha, a vase of flowers, or anything else that assists you in achieving a state of serenity.

The next step is to choose a position in which you will meditate; however, regardless of whatever posture you choose, you should be sure to get a quality zafu. A zafu is a spherical meditation cushion that is particularly intended to let you effortlessly settle on the ground in any stance you choose so that you may concentrate properly.

If, on the other hand, you do not intend to make any such investment at this time, you may take any cushion, soft or firm, that will assist you in sitting comfortably on the ground. It is possible to relax without using a cushion if you are able to do so for two to five minutes at the beginning of the exercise.

Following the 7 point Buddhist meditation practice, there are 6 different stances that one might settle into before beginning meditation.

The Pose of the Quarter Lotus

Place your zafu or any other cushion on top of your yoga mat once you have spread it out on the ground. You should be able to sit on it with your legs comfortably crossed and both of your feet resting just below the knee or thigh of the opposite side. This is the greatest and simplest posture for beginners since it is very easy to perform and does not need you to put any excessive strain on yourself. It is also the most straightforward pose to describe.

The Lotus Half

This is a simpler version of the complete lotus stance that you may try. If you find that placing both feet on the opposite thighs makes the quarter lotus posture too difficult for you, you shouldn't do that. Instead, just cross your legs and place either one of your feet on the thigh or leg on the opposing side. You have the option of tucking your other foot under your upper leg or letting it rest directly below either your thigh or knee.

Completed lotus position

It is arguable that this is the ideal position for achieving perfect stability throughout the exercise and keeping one's concentration strong. However, since it is little difficult to maintain, many individuals have difficulty practicing the full lotus position and instead begin by adopting the half lotus stance or the quarter lotus pose. This is because it is slightly difficult to keep.

To put it into effect, you should first choose a comfortable sitting position on the zafu or even directly on the floor, then cross both of your legs so that each of your feet is resting comfortably on the top of the opposite thigh, and then sit up straight.

The Burmese Pose.

There is no use in trying to force yourself to sit on the ground with both legs crossed if it is too difficult for you to do so; there is also no reason to push yourself to hold that position if it is really tough. You will eventually get there and acquire the stability, concentration, and flexibility you need to correctly practice the many lotus positions, but for now you may attempt the straightforward Burmese stance. You will ultimately get there and attain the stability, focus, and flexibility you need to properly practice the other lotus poses.

Relax in a comfortable seated position with both feet flat on the ground while adopting the easy posture. Take a thick blanket and fold it to make this process simpler, or you may use your zafu or any other cushion with a hard surface to sit on instead. You may either sit on the edge of the zafu or the blanket, and then extend your legs in front of you so that they are stretched out on the ground.

First, your shins should be crossed, and then your knees should be widening. Fold your legs in toward your chest by sliding your feet carefully underneath their matching opposite knees and then gently folding your legs inwards. Put your feet in a relaxed position so that their outer edges may rest on the floor and their inner arches can rest just under the shins of the opposite leg.

Making the Decision to Hold On

The ladies raise their voices and begin to sob once again. On the other hand, this time it is not the possibility of parting ways that gives them grief, but rather hearing the illnesses that Naomi is going through. Orpah makes the decision to respect the wishes of her mother-in-law. Orpah weeps as she travels back to her hometown of Bethlehem, having been persuaded by Naomi's negative views that there is a brighter future in Moab than in Bethlehem. She decides to go with the option that seems to be the most rational one. She goes back to the place where she feels most at home, among her people and her gods, and from there she can start the process of rebuilding her life.

On the other side, Ruth is adamant about not going back. She clings to Naomi like a terrified young child, afraid to release go in case her mother-in-law vanishes. She fears that if she does, her mother-in-law will no longer exist. Ruth makes the decision to leave her homeland and start a new life in a different country. She has neither the supply nor the protection that she needs since there is no man present. In addition to all of this, she is travelling to Israel, a country that has a history of treating Moabites with disdain. Bethlehem presents her with a challenging and uncertain future, but Moab assures her of a future of comfort and consistency. She decides to hold to it despite the fact that there is no valid justification for it and that there is no valid explanation for it. Naomi, exasperated, cites Orpah as a precedent for the situation. Now that reason has failed her, she tries to convince him by appealing to Orpah's position as the option that is both reasonable and obedient. Naomi is at a complete loss to fathom the motivation for this woman's insistence on spending time with her.

The choice that Ruth has made is unintelligible due to the fact that she has made an unreasonable and puzzling choice. The fact that Ruth has chosen to cling to Naomi stems from the affection she has for her. This is a love that defies all explanations and explanations. This kind of love is beyond comprehension. Love does not need any justification. Love is a selfless act that makes an unshakable commitment to the other person. The Hebrew word that is translated here as "clung" is the same word that is translated as "cleave" in Genesis 2:24, where it is used to characterize the institution of marriage. This is the strength that Ruth's love for Naomi, her jaded and resentful mother-in-law, possesses. As her name implies, Ruth is a loyal and trustworthy companion. In this, we see a glimpse of the love that God has for us that is reflected in Jesus. According to John 15:13, "there is no greater love than that someone should lay down their life for their friends." Why does God love miserable sinners enough to send his son to die for them? Is it due of the excellent actions we do, the moral character we uphold, or the value we bring to God as a result of our lives? No! Because of his love, God makes the decision to stay close to those who sin. In 1 John 4:8, the Bible says that God loves us because he loves, and that God loves because he is love.

THE SECOND CHAPTER

WHAT Is the Practice of Kriya Yoga?

Both kri and ya refer to the vital life force that is inside everyone of us. Every time we take a breath, we bring more energy from our spirit into our bodies. Kriya yoga is all about accessing the energy of the soul via a certain breathing technique that has a rhythmic pattern. Always keep in mind that the rhythm of our breathing is very closely related to the condition of our thoughts. When our mental state changes, there is a corresponding shift in the pattern of breathing that we exhibit, as may be seen by careful study. It is also true that the opposite of this phenomena and vice versa is true. We are able to bring about a shift in our mental state by adopting a certain rhythmic pattern of breathing.

I take it that kriya refers to a certain kind of breathing?

Not at all, not at all. Kriya yoga is a meditation system that involves preparing the mind for the practice of a certain breathing method that has the ability to broaden the scope of one's consciousness. Lord Shiva himself, Adinath, is said to be the first instructor of kriya yoga. Kriya yoga is also the name given to the method of meditation that Lord Krishna recommends in the Bhagavad Gita. Recent legend states that Mahavtar Babaji passed on this knowledge to Lahiri Mahashay. Lahiri Mahashay was his student, and he instructed her in the 108 kriya yoga practice. These methods were reserved for those interested in advanced study. However, there is a basic kriya yoga practice that is appropriate for beginners.

Is telling the truth therefore a strategy?

In no uncertain terms, no. Techniques of breathing that function and expand our minds may be attributed to having an attitude or philosophy of mind that is true. The act of preparing for meditation is in some ways more challenging than meditation itself.

When it comes to meditation, why is preparation so very important?

See, the typical state of our mind is one that is mostly always preoccupied with ideas. Thoughts constantly come and go. In a nutshell, we ruminate in our thoughts the vast majority of the time. Other than our ideas, there is no other aspect of life that we have. The sphere of energy that ideas roll across is what we refer to as consciousness. The waves that move over the surface of awareness are analogous to our thoughts. In order to increase the size of that awareness, we will first need to still the flow of ideas that is occurring over it. Additionally, thoughts have both a destination and a movement, in addition to a profound component of attachment. During the process of getting ready to meditate, there should be a firm conviction that we have to go beyond the typical range of our thoughts and that we should make an effort to broaden the scope of our awareness.

I'd like to share with you the tale of how I first became interested in kriya yoga. When I was a medical student ten years ago, one of my Jewish friends gave me the book Autobiography of a Yogi. It was at that time that I first became interested in yoga. As soon as I began reading the book, I was presented with the concept of kriya yoga for the very first time.

After some time, I received diksha from reliable sources, and over the course of many years, via the consistent use of kriya yoga meditation, I came to understand its wonderful science.

Through the practice of Kriya Yoga, we come to understand that the potential of the human mind is very vast. If this mind is not trained in the appropriate manner, then it will become our biggest adversary. On the other hand, if this mind is grown and enlarged in a specific way via the practices of meditation, then it will become the finest diamond in this world. The emotional anguish that we all endure is to blame for all of the chaos that exists in our world. If by the practice of meditation this mind is able to grow more expansive, then this mind will become the greatest paradise on earth.

The Benefits That Meditation Can Have On The Body

In Devekut meditation, you do not use words; rather, you just use your mind and the power of thought. On the other hand, when you meditate using the divine verb, you employ the word that is holy in all kinds of magic and in all faiths.

Meditation employing the verb, making use of the creative larynx, and focusing on the energy vortex above the larynx that governs the glands of the human body that are situated in the throat has a significant effect on our spirits.

Mantras are defined as the repeating of words while utilizing the voice in Indian culture, however in Kabbalah, it is understood to be the meditation of the divine verb. During this meditation,

Kabbalists utilize holy language and the names of celestial beings.

Meditation that involves utilizing one's voice is proactive and has an effect not just on earth but also on the universe. The heavenly verb is revered, and the act of using it has an effect on the coherence of the cosmos. This, in turn, helps to shed light not only on the world at large but also on all of mankind, nature, and most importantly, the life of the meditator and the life of his family.

The holy verb that is expressed during meditation causes the body to vibrate, which integrates the soul with the physical body and, as a result of this bridge, passes energy to the glandular system of the human body. This meditation operates on the glands by means of vibration, having an effect on the most fundamental level of the cells, the chain of atoms, and therefore radiating across the whole of the body. The glands have a significant impact on the human being.

System of Endocrine Hormones

The group of glands known as the endocrine system are responsible for the generation of hormones. These hormones are then secreted into the bloodstream, where they circulate throughout the body until they reach the organs that they are intended to regulate. The endocrine system, in conjunction with the, is responsible for coordinating all of the processes of our body. (1) A collection of nerve cells called the hypothalamus, which is situated at the base of the brain, is responsible for integrating these two different systems.

The endocrine system's glands and their functions

The pituitary gland, the thyroid, the parathyroid glands, the thymus, the adrenal glands, the pancreas, and the sexual glands are all examples of endocrine glands that may be found in various areas of the body.

The hypophysis of

In the middle of the top of the skull, just under the brain, is where you'll find the pituitary gland. It is responsible for the production of a number of hormones, including the growth hormone. Because it is responsible for stimulating the operation of other glands in our body, such as the thyroid and the sexual glands, it is sometimes referred to as the "master gland." This hormone is responsible for both gigantism (excessive growth) and dwarfism (inadequate growth), depending on how much of it is produced. The antidiuretic (ADH) hormone is still another hormone that is generated by the pituitary gland.

This hormone is a chemical that enables the body to save water during the process of excretion (the creation of urine).

The thyroid

The thyroid gland, which may be found in the neck, is responsible for producing the hormone thyroxine. This hormone regulates the pace at which cells in the body metabolize their food, as well as the body's temperature, growth, and rate of heartbeat.

Hyperthyroidism, also known as an overactive thyroid function, speeds up the whole metabolic process. This causes the heart to beat more quickly, the body temperature to rise beyond normal, and the individual to lose weight as a result of expending more energy. Because of the increased pressure that the blood is under during circulation, this circumstance makes it more likely that cardiovascular problems may manifest themselves. If it is not treated, it might result in the emergence of exophthalmos, which is characterized by protruding eyes, as well as a goiter, which is an enlargement of the neck.

Hypothyroidism is a condition that occurs when the thyroid produces less thyroxin and performs less effectively. Because of this, the metabolism slows down, leading to certain areas of the body to swell; the heart beats more slowly, the blood circulates more slowly, the person expends less energy, has a tendency to put on weight, and the person's physical and mental reactions become slower; also, goiter may develop if the condition is left untreated.

Parathyroid glands

The parathyroid glands are a group of four tiny glands that are situated beneath the thyroid and are responsible for the production of parathyroid hormone. This hormone controls the levels of calcium and phosphorus that are present in the blood. The reduction in production of this hormone leads to a lower concentration of calcium in the blood, which in turn causes the muscles to forcefully contract. Tetany is the name given to this symptom since it is quite similar to what happens to persons who have tetanus. The increased synthesis of this hormone, in turn, causes a portion of the body's calcium to be transferred into the blood, which in turn causes the bones to become weakened and brittle.

The herb thyme

The thymus may be found in the chest cavity in between the lungs. It is responsible for the production of a hormone that plays an active role in the newborn's body's fight against infections. During this stage, it has a noticeable volume and will continue to develop regularly up until puberty, when it will begin to atrophy. When it reaches maturity, its size shrinks, and its functions become less important.

Adrenal gland(s)

The adrenal glands are found directly above the kidneys, and they are responsible for the production of adrenaline, which is a hormone that gets the body ready for action. The effects of adrenaline on the body are as follows: • Tachycardia: the heart races and pushes more blood to the legs and arms, increasing the ability to run or to exalt itself in tense situations; • Increased respiratory rate and blood glucose rate, releasing more energy for cells; • Contraction of the blood vessels in the skin, so that the body sends more blood to the skeletal muscles, causing us to appear "pale with fright" and also "frozen with fear."

The pancreas

The pancreas is a mixed gland because in addition to producing hormones (insulin and glucagon), it also generates pancreatic juice. This juice is then secreted into the body, where it plays a vital function.

Insulin is a hormone that regulates how much glucose is stored in the liver in the form of glycogen and how much glucose is allowed to enter cells (where it will be utilized to generate energy). Diabetes is a condition that is characterized by high blood glucose levels (hyperglycemia), which may be caused by either a lack of or a poor production of insulin.

Insulin has the opposite effect on the body that glucagon does. If a person spends several hours without eating, their blood sugar level will drop significantly, and they may develop hypoglycemia. Hypoglycemia causes feelings of weakness and dizziness, and it is the most common cause of passing out in these situations. In this instance, the pancreas generates glucagon, which works on the liver to stimulate the "breakdown" of glycogen into glucose molecules. This process is triggered by the pancreas' production of the hormone glucagon. In order to get the blood sugar level back up to normal, glucose is finally administered.

An Introduction to Meditation is Discussed in Chapter 1.

Sitting quietly in a calm setting while maintaining a reflective frame of mind is just one aspect of the practice of meditation. It requires forming connections, genuine ties to the things you do on a daily basis. Meditation is an age-old practice that consists of sitting in quiet reflection while focusing one's attention on a particular idea or object. When you engage in a practice like meditation, you'll find that it helps you see and comprehend things more clearly than you ever have before. When you meditate, you take stock of everything that is going on in your life and in you as a whole at the same time. You are going to realize that in the past, you had a difficult time comprehending yourself. On the other hand, you may learn more about yourself with the assistance of meditation. It contributes to your personal growth and reveals to you a more positive outlook on life.

It is not true that in order to learn how to meditate, you need to be a religious person who observes religious rituals. Although many religious traditions include components of contemplative practices, this does not mean that in order to learn how to meditate, you need to be a religious person. You are free to begin at any point along your journey and to educate yourself independently.

You will be able to get a more profound understanding of who you are and who you have the potential to become by practicing meditation. Your genuine personality and the areas of expertise in which you excel will become more apparent to you as time passes. When you meditate, you open up new pathways of awareness in both your heart and your intellect, which ultimately leads to a more satisfying existence. When you gain awareness, you begin to completely notice every event and milestone that is occurring in your life while it is happening. This allows you to truly appreciate the journey that you are on.

The following is a list of some additional advantages of meditation:

You may improve your knowledge of the mind and your ability to utilize it effectively via the practice of meditation. You are able to alleviate some of the tension and worry that is present in your life by practicing meditation.

One of the purposes of meditation is to assist a person in better comprehending herself or herself. You are one of a kind in your own special manner, yet everyone else shares their humanity.

Your perspective will expand as you practice meditation. It motivates you to look inside for the resources and creativity you already possess. When you meditate, you may experience feelings that drive you to squeeze as much value as possible out of each day.

Everyone strives for mental calmness, and meditating regularly may help you achieve this goal while also opening up opportunities for a rich and fulfilling life. You will also find that your sleep is more rejuvenating and peaceful.

A person who meditates is able to make the most of any chance, no matter how seemingly little it may seem.

The body may become more relaxed via the practice of meditation. When a person is in a calm condition, it helps their whole body since it indicates that their heart rate and blood pressure are stable, that they have excellent posture, and that they have greater energy. When you meditate, the waves of your brain are in a different condition than when they are when you are walking or when you are sleeping. The mind and the body become one when one practices meditation. And most importantly, you may teach yourself to remove yourself from problematic and stressful ideas, which will allow you to improve your attention.

How to Get Ready for Your Meditation Session

If you want to get the most out of your meditation practice, you should be familiar with the following guidelines first:

Reflect on your current situation.

You need to set aside some time to reflect on who you are and the principles that guide your daily life. You may start by taking an inventory of your life as it is right now. Start by examining the way in which you are now conducting your life. Is everything turning out the way you envisioned it? Take a close look at the life that you have fashioned for yourself. Have you zeroed down on what really interests you? Do you put forth too much effort? Find out what your true priorities are and focus on them. Think about the things that are most important to you. Taking stock is comparable to organizing one's closet. You get to choose what you want to preserve and what you want to get rid of in this scenario.

Find Out Where You've Been

The journey that is life is often used as a metaphor. Make use of this concept as you get ready to meditate so that you may examine your life in more detail. You may scribble down how far you have come in life, or you could design a map instead. Both options are available to you. You are able to include significant milestones in your biography, such as friends, family, and significant events that have occurred in your life. Now, ask yourself this question: has it been a difficult slog uphill all the way or has it been smooth sailing? If you do this before you truly devote yourself to a meditation practice on a regular basis, it will help you become more aware of the direction you want your life to go. Keep in mind that we all leave traces in the past; thus, do not be frightened to look back at the tracks that you have left. If you want to realize where you are in life today, it is essential to take a look back at where you came from.

Keep a log or a diary.

Additionally, it would be beneficial if you kept a meditation diary for the purpose of serving as a record for yourself. Consider each post in your journal as a photograph that will be added to an album that you will be able to browse over and reflect on in the years to come.

You should keep a record of the many types of meditations that you have attempted, as well as make a note of how each one went and whether or not there were any difficulties along the road. It is recommended that you make it a routine to take down some notes immediately after each meditation session, since this is when your thoughts are considered to be the clearest and your memory the most recent. But keep in mind that you should simply scribble down brief notes. Do not force oneself to keep a notebook or make it a duty to do so.

It Is Time to Begin Our Journey

It's possible that once you've spent some time taking stock of your life, planning out your path, and reminding yourself to write things down, you'll feel like you're ready to start learning how to meditate. Now is the moment to make the first move and start over in life; the time to take action has come. The decision to begin meditating marks a significant turning point in one's life. It is a fresh approach to the future that will lead to a higher understanding of one's own life and of the world around them.

How To Get Rid Of Stress Through Meditation

The human body is predisposed to have a response in the event of stress. Either we choose to run away from what is generating the stress in our lives or we choose to remain and combat it. On the other hand, the consequences might be disastrous if we keep our bodies in a perpetual state of "fight or flight." When one practices meditation, the body goes through the complete reverse of what is described above. The condition of tranquility and a sense of emotional well-being are both enhanced via the practice of meditation. The effects of stress on the body may be reversed via the practice of meditation.

When you first start meditating, you will notice that the tension is being replaced with a sense of tranquility. You will get the sensation that you are once again able to think clearly, and that your mind is not clogged with a thousand different things that are weighing it down. You will notice that you are better equipped to deal with stress when it occurs, and that your responses are different once you have entered that heightened feeling of mental awareness. You will also find that you are able to withstand stressful situations for longer.

Meditation has been shown to reduce the rate of one's heartbeat, raise the degree of happiness one experiences, improve one's ability to sleep, and remove many of the negative side effects and symptoms that are associated with stress. When you meditate, you sharpen your awareness of your mind and engage in much more profound thought. We are able to raise our awareness of stress, how we adjust to that stress and how we react to it, as well as how we worry and the reasons behind our worrying. Once we have achieved the mental state of meditation, we are in a position to change the manner in which we react to worries by putting a non-threatening idea in front of them.

The Methodology Behind Meditating

When you first start meditating, you will experience the following benefits:

Mind Calming: Once you start meditating, you'll notice that your mind starts to calm down, and you'll have the impression that the stressful things in your life have disappeared. Your internal monologue is silent, as it should be, and you shouldn't try to change that. It is far simpler to state something than it is to really carry it through, and doing so will need practice.

Be present in the moment: You just are unable to keep your attention on things that occurred the day before yesterday, three weeks ago, or six months ago. You have no control over the events that will take place tomorrow or in a year from now. You absolutely have to be present in the here and now in order for meditation to work for you. You are only allowed to concentrate on what is happening in the here and now. You have to make the most of each moment, and when it's over, you have to accept that it's over and let it go. Proceed to the next experience that life has to offer, and be sure to enjoy it to the fullest while you still can.

Transform the state of consciousness you are in: You will be able to modify your state of mind and achieve a level of awareness that is midway between being awake and asleep after you have mastered the ability to still the mind and be present in the here and now. When you reach the advanced level of meditation, you will notice a rise in the amount of brain activity in regions associated with happy thoughts and feelings.

The Fundamentals Of Meditation: An Outline And Guide To Getting Started

Meditation will bring you a great deal of benefit, as was mentioned in the previous chapters of this book. However, before to beginning your meditation practice, you should first consider what it is that you want to gain from it. Do you want to experience more ease and tranquility in your life? Do you wish to gain perspective and develop your intuitive abilities? Do you long to have a mind that is both more alert and more focused? Do you want to have a greater awareness of both the acts and ideas you take? Do you want to get over the mental scars and baggage that you've been dragging around for so many years?

You need to have a crystal clear idea of what you want to gain out of your meditation practice in order to get the most out of it. This will allow you to practice the most effective meditation method that will help you achieve your objective.

There are several approaches to meditation.

Being mindful The practice of Meditation – This is one of the most common approaches used in the practice of meditation. It is a Western meditation technique that does not adhere to any one religious group. The goal of mindfulness meditation is to train one's attention and awareness to be more present in the here and now.

Meditation on Mantras is an old practice that has its roots in the Vedic culture. Mantra meditation follows this heritage. Practitioners of this kind of meditation are able to concentrate their attention on a mantra.

Meditation of the Kundalini kind is practiced with the intention of reawakening the Kundalini energy, which, when activated, bestows the practitioner with enhanced insight and intuition, as well as the capacity to heal and access psychic skills.

Heart Rhythm Meditation is a kind of meditation that places an emphasis on the heart chakra and teaches practitioners to develop a greater capacity for compassion. This kind of meditation also assists you in letting go of your feelings of despair and fear.

Reflective Meditation is a kind of meditation that focuses on answering more significant questions about oneself and one's place in the world, such as "What is my purpose?" and "Who am I?" and "How can I help others?"

Visualization is another name for creative meditation, which is another name for creative meditation. This style of meditation is designed to help you attract synchronicity in your life, which will assist you in achieving your objectives and fulfilling your desires. Your feeling of appreciation, humility, bravery, and tenderness will all increase as a result of practicing this form of visualization.

This style of meditation is called chakra meditation, and its goal is to open the many chakras or energy centres in the body.

Instructions on How to Begin
It is time for you to start meditating now that you are familiar with the many approaches to this practice. The following is a list of the actions that you need to do in order to get started with your meditation practice:

You need to choose a location for your meditation practice in which you won't be interrupted or diverted in any way. It is necessary for you to choose a peaceful spot, either in your bedroom or in your yard, in which you may meditate. You have to make sure that you choose a location that is pleasant to be in and that has the appropriate level of temperature and humidity.

Before beginning your meditation practice, you should dress in clothing that are extremely easy on the body. Make sure that you are wearing clothing that is not tight and is made of a fabric that is not hot. Wearing clothing that is too constricting may cause you to feel uncomfortable, which in turn will distract you from your meditation practice.

It's best not to eat anything in the hour or so before up to your meditation session. Nevertheless, you should also make sure that you are not famished. Both hunger and fullness will make you uncomfortable and have the potential to divert your attention away from your practice. However, it is essential to drink enough water throughout the day.

Take a seat on a chair or a cushion, whatever would make you feel the most at ease.

When you are trying to meditate, you need to ensure that you are completely at ease. You have to sit in a posture that allows your back to be straight. It is imperative that you ensure that your back is in a neutral position. You need to make sure that your shoulders are pulled back and that your chest is open at all times. When you meditate in a state of tranquility, you get additional benefits from the practice. Even while meditation helps you feel more relaxed and tranquil, it might be challenging to practice when you are concerned with a variety of challenges and activities. It is recommended that you do something soothing before beginning the meditation process. You may go for a little stroll around the park, stretch, read an engaging book, watch an entertaining movie, or even take a relaxing bath.

You may practice meditation with either your eyes open or closed. There is no need for you to adhere to a certain structure or position when you are first beginning to meditate. The important thing is to choose an activity that you can do easily. If you are uncomfortable in your current position, try switching positions every so often.

Take some long, slow breaths. When you meditate, you want to make sure that your breaths are both regular and deep since this will establish the pattern for your practice. Keep in mind that you should concentrate on your breath.

Listen to some soothing music as you meditate. You may find a lot of relaxing music for meditation that you can get from the internet and utilize while you are practicing.

Create a routine for your meditation sessions. You need to commit to meditating at a certain time every day. You can't just count on having "free time," you have to make a commitment to meditating every day. When you are just getting started with meditation, it is recommended that you meditate for five to ten minutes at a time. As you become better, you'll be able to play for longer periods of time.

You need to give yourself some time and be patient as you wait for it to come to you. At first, meditation may seem difficult, therefore you will need patience and determination to get through it.

You need to make meditation a consistent part of your routine. You will not be able to experience the advantages of meditation if you just meditate once or twice. You need to make meditation a routine practice that you do every day.

You will experience the most advantages of meditation if you choose a meditation practice that is tailored to your unique characteristics and requirements. You need to settle on the idea that you will meditate and give your complete attention to the practice before you can begin. Meditation isn't like other activities where you can just try it once or twice and call it good. Your daily routine and your life in general might benefit from the practice of meditation. It is a never-ending process of unwinding, coming to know oneself better, and coming into one with the divine.

Both the spleen and the larynx are important to the creative process and operate together. Both eyesight and intellect are connected to the Solar Plexus, which is also known as the Third Eye. The dimensions will be expressed by the heart and coronary structures. Each chakra will, at a reduced frequency, nevertheless convey the function that it was designed to express. The inability to absorb, transform, or integrate different energy frequencies is another factor that may contribute to disease. When energy attempts to enter a chakra but is prevented from doing so, it will look for other ways to express itself, for as via psychological detachment. If, on the other hand, there is already energy present in a chakra but that energy is manifested in a destructive way, it will ultimately show up as bodily difficulties.

The connection between Chromotherapy and the Chakras

Chromotherapy is one of the methods that may be used to replenish our energy centers, also known as chakras. We were able to produce an exterior harmony by shining lights of varying hues on each of them. At this point, it should be obvious that the way we take care of our chakras is entirely up to us. No matter what approach we adopt, we will always see an instant improvement in all three domains (physical, emotional, and mental), but this state of well-being will only be maintained for as long as we focus on our own health.

The use of a strobe light is an efficient technique for balancing the chakras. This light has the unique property of being able to blink at varied rates, and by making use of a variety of filters and colors, each chakra will progressively speed up as a result of this light. As a result of this enhancement, it will be able to purify and restore its own energy. When I talk about cleansing, what I mean is that our emotions, bad ideas, or self-demands are growing worse, and their original hue is becoming darker. The following is a list of the chakras and the colors associated with them in the ether:

Color of the Coronary Chakra: Violet

Color of the Third Eye Chakra: white

Color of the Laryngeal Chakra: Turquoise

Green represents the Heart Chakra.

Color of the Solar Plexus Chakra: Orange

Color of the Splenic Chakra: Yellow

The first chakra, red

To further illustrate our points, let's look at an example.

Vishuddha, the Fifth Chakra.

The color is a sky blue.

Crystals include Celestina and Aquamarine.

Place: in the throat

The fifth chakra is in charge of our ability to be creative in its broadest sense. Because it is a fact that not everyone in this world is meant to be an artist, even if he has a good balance in this Chakra, the term "creativity" refers to more than only art when it is discussed here.

If you are an entrepreneur, you will have a "bombing" of ideas that will lead your company to success. If you are a housewife, you will have enough "spark" to make the routine something special (serving food is not the same as decorating the table with flowers and details to make that moment unique and comfortable). Creativity develops in any field in which we work. If you are an entrepreneur, you will have a "bombing" of ideas that will lead your company to success. In each case, creative thinking is required for the completion of any task.

Because the throat is the location of our fifth Chakra, it will also regulate our voice. However, it will not only regulate our physical voice; it will also regulate our inner voice, which struggles to express its ideas without fear of other people, without fear of not being accepted, and without fear that the people around us do not share our ideals. When we do this, we are telling the truth, our truth.

We solely share our ideas here, and we are not concerned with persuading anybody else or forcing our way of thinking; rather, we simply engage in an idea exchange out of a desire to express ourselves. Here, there is no fervor or fanaticism. You will be attracted by knowledge, you will ask yourself questions about life, but you will not identify with any nor will you criticize others, because first and foremost there will be the understanding of each of them, the what of each way, and far from rejecting them, you will open to know them. The philosophical and religious currents enter this point of expression and creativity. The "flashes of light" will come to your thoughts, you will begin to answer all of your questions, or the answers will begin to reach you via other methods (books, movies, facts in your life, etc.). This will happen when you are surrounded by an unending number of questions about the mysteries of life.

When we learn to strike a balance between our outward expression and our internal monologue, we also gain the ability to master our stage fright, or the feeling of unease that comes over us whenever we are required to deliver a speech in front of an audience. We will be able to master this anxiety by channeling our nerves into "creating the best speech." It is not about suffocating or concealing our energy; rather, it is about working with it and approaching it from a creative standpoint.

The transition to the fifth Chakra requires a significant expansion of one's awareness. This is the first Chakra in the higher levels, and it represents the melding of one's particular consciousness with that of the greater cosmos. We are no longer concerned with classifying ourselves according to a political ideology, a religious belief, or anything else; instead, we opt to make choices based on an independent point of view. This results in thought that is both original and personal. Our perspective of the world broadens, and we share that growth with others in the hopes that it may inspire others to do the same. Any philosophical or theological movement extends farther than obedience or culture, and as a result, we learn to appreciate the beauty that each of them has. Despite the fact that we do not share any of their characteristics, we respect them. There are varying points of view that need to be defended, but we are in agreement. When we do this, the consciousness of the universe flows through us. We are able to locate the middle ground in any ideological system. We are able to recognize them, and nothing external is forced upon us.

A Brief Explanation Of Psychic Capabilities

Everyone has the potential to make use of their psychic powers, regardless of whether or not they are conscious of this fact. This is due to the fact that everyone of us is an eternal and limitless being of energy that is made up of a piece of the cosmos that is referred to as your soul. Because there are many con artists in the world who take advantage of people with their "powers," also known as deceptions, the majority of us have been conditioned to think that intuitive and psychic talents do not genuinely exist. This is due to the fact that many individuals claim to have these abilities. People who are desperate or needy have access to a strong instrument that they are able to utilize to their own benefit, and that instrument is the employment of a mental trick. The general public has developed a healthy skepticism of the possibility of psychic abilities as a result of their interactions with the individuals described above, whether in the media or in real life.

One excellent illustration of this is the possibility that you had more psychic experiences when you were younger. Children have a more direct connection to the energies that surround them, as well as a greater degree of purity as a result of their lack of life experiences. Because of this, it is conceivable that you were able to see energy or words from another realm, hear them in your dreams, or hear them directly. The adults in your life, having been socialized to think that psychic connections do not exist, most likely laughed at your experiences or tried to rationalize them away. This is because society has been conditioned to believe that psychic connections do not exist.

On the other hand, there are some individuals who have the good fortune to be able to learn about these skills from members of their family or from other caregivers. These people are very lucky. They will support and educate the linked kid so that they are better able to cope with all of the unusual experiences that will cause most others to believe them to be insane. These are the people who have a strong belief that there are rare other energies that exist outside of ourselves, and they are the people who have a strong belief that there are rare other energies that exist outside of ourselves.

You may have had an encounter in which you communicated with a spirit or ghost that was not there in physical form, but you were able to see them and interact with them as if they were real. For instance, you may have been able to see them and play with them. If you were to tell your parents about this ghost, it is probable that they would not have been able to see them themselves; so, rather than accepting you at your word, they would likely explain it by stating that you had an imaginary friend. This is a more acceptable idea in society, while it may seem far-fetched to some people, the majority of people will not think the youngster is insane for making up a buddy to spend their time with since it is a common practice.

Because this experience was not stated in the correct manner, you have probably begun to feel that this spirit was all a part of your imagination as well - that you made it in your mind. This is probably the case because this experience was not properly defined. On the other hand, due of your childlike perspective and general lack of mistrust toward the outside world, it is quite possible that you were able to notice things that other people were unable to perceive. The wonder and enchantment of the world, as seen through the eyes of a kid, is typically no longer there as the child grows older and becomes more preoccupied with the calamities and stresses of adult life, such as romantic relationships and professional obligations. A child's existence does not include these things, and as a result, their spirit is more pure, which enables these higher energies to enter through with more ease.

Even if you were unable to maintain this link as you grew into an adult, it does not indicate that you are unable to use this talent in the future. In point of fact, anybody of any age may train and strive to enhance their psychic skills; all that is required is a significant amount of self-love, physical activity, and patience on their part. One of the most important things you can do to do this is to shift your viewpoint and believe that these talents are a kind of fraud or a lie. They are nothing of the like, and you do not have to depend on what your society and the media have taught you to believe in order to make decisions about what you believe.

When you make use of your psychic abilities, you are going to experience an increase in sensitivity in one or more of the following aspects of the energy world: your sense of taste, your sense of feeling, your sense of hearing, your vision, and your intuition. As a matter of fact, the field of psychology lacks a definitive definition of what it means to be "normal," and as a result, determining what constitutes "normal" is something that must be done using a scale that is unique to the individual. There are many different degrees of intensity associated with these heightened sensations. The more you practice, you will notice that the intensity will increase as you come back in touch with your intuition and psychic talents. This is because the intensity is directly related to how well you have been practicing.

It is essential to point out that since you will have a new way of experiencing the world, you may suffer increased feelings of isolation due to the fact that you will not be able to speak to just anyone about the things that you have gone through in your life. On the other hand, there are a great number of other individuals who, like you, have been practicing for a variety of lengths of time and with whom you will be able to share your experiences, as well as get advice or direction. If you are able to engage these extrasensory aspects of ourselves, you will develop a deeper comprehension of both your own identity and the environment in which you find yourself. As you go farther into the underworld, your experiences will get more strange, to the point that you may have trouble putting them into words. As you strengthen your connection with yourself and the energy of the other realms, all of this is a natural and expected aspect of the experience.

The Importance Of Practicing Meditation For Five Minutes

Chronic stress in the workplace has emerged as a key contributor to employee mortality, a topic that was touched on briefly in the introduction. In an effort to convince you of the need of incorporating meditation into your hectic lifestyle, it is important that we first get an understanding of how perilous this unseen adversary really is.

People who overextend themselves physically and mentally are more likely to experience symptoms of stress, which may appear in a variety of ways. Let's take a look at various manifestations according to the features that they may display, which are as follows:

Sensitive to feelings

At work, a person who is stressed may give off the impression of being too emotional and melancholy than they normally would. When it comes to their job, they have a tendency to become more sensitive and angry overall, as well as dissatisfied in themselves on a growing scale if things do not go the way they want them to. They often engage in solitary behavior and have extreme mood swings that are characterized by a wide range of emotions. They are far less confident in themselves, and as a result, their levels of motivation are much lower. The mere fact that they isolate themselves is not due to the fact that they are introverts by nature; rather, it is due to the fact that they have a persistent underlying issue that causes them to behave in a manner that is analogous to what they exhibit.

The mind

When it comes to the world of the mind, persons who are racked with chronic stress are actually the most indecisive and confused people. They are unable to concentrate nearly as effectively as they normally would, and their memories are also not as crisp as they normally would be.

the behavior of

A person who is suffering from chronic stress will display a number of behavioral changes, such as irregular eating patterns and a twitchy, anxiety. These changes may be caused by the cumulative effects of the stress. They may even turn to excessive smoking or drinking as a means of coping with the elevated levels of stress that they find themselves being exposed to. In addition, it is quite likely that they will arrive at the workplace later than normal and leave earlier than usual, on average. This is because they will be leaving the office sooner than usual.

If you discover that you are experiencing the majority of the aforementioned symptoms, it is likely that you might benefit from the 5-minute meditation methods that we will go over in the latter part of this book. Aside from these very evident indicators that one is experiencing too much stress, there are other bodily impacts of stress that may present themselves later on as well, and you will want to make every effort to avoid giving in to those effects if at all possible. Let's have a look at them so that we can get a better understanding of why it's so important to avoid generating long-term stress in our lives!

Meditation While Assuming Various Positions

Since you now have a thorough understanding of the mechanics of meditation, you are now prepared to personalize the practice as a whole. If you are one of those persons who find it difficult to sit down for extended periods of time, or if you are merely exploring variations on the standard approaches, then this chapter was written just for you. In this section, we will talk about how we can meditate not just while sitting still but also while standing, walking, and even laying down.

Meditation while walking

The practice of keeping a still mind during walking meditation is a wonderful way to move between maintaining a still mind when the body is stationary and maintaining a still mind while engaged in all of your other activities. Long walks have always provided me with a sense of calm and relaxation, so you can imagine my delight when I discovered that I could practice meditation even while I was walking.

Walking meditation may be performed in one of two ways: either by walking in a circular pattern on a predetermined route or by just going for a walk. The first approach is more effective at calming the mind, while the second is more practical in situations where you don't have access to a route that is free from disturbances and along which you may stroll in both directions without arousing the attention or worry of other people.

Pick a route that is either 20 or 70 paces long and stay on the level. In an ideal world, it ought to be a direct route. Try spending a minute standing at one end and observing how your body feels in terms of its alignment and whether or not it is balanced. After then, direct your focus on the act of breathing. Take a few long, deep breaths in and out, and then concentrate your attention on the feelings that arise from the breath in a particular region of the body. You should breathe in such a manner that the location you've picked may become more relaxed, open, and revitalized as a result of your actions. Do you remember the exercises that we went through for your breathing? Now is the time to put them into practice once again, but this time while you are walking.

You should walk at a regular speed or just a touch more slowly than usual. When you walk, don't look about at everything. Keep your inner attention focused upon the location in the body that you've selected to focus on during the whole trip.

When you have reached the opposite end of the road, you should pause for a little while to check that your attention is still focused on the location that you have picked. If it has been lost, you should try to find it and bring it back.

After then, spin around so that you are facing the other way and walk back to where you began while keeping your attention on the location you picked.

Why Should One Meditate According To Buddhist Principles?

The greatest advantage of practicing Buddhist meditation is that it takes one closer to bliss, which was discussed at length at the beginning of this book. Although it's natural to want to be happy, there's something that outweighs that desire more than anything else: the need for serenity.

To be happy is to experience an emotion, and just like other emotions, happiness is fleeting. Nobody can always be smiling and laughing all the time. The feeling of happiness is analogous to the appearance of a cloud, which then either fades away or reforms into a new form. The only thing that is everlasting is the inner calm that comes with attaining enlightenment. while we have reached this higher level of awareness and have established ourselves there, we are able to feel inner peace even while we are experiencing negative emotions such as rage or despair.

Because everything else that we encounter in our lives is ephemeral, the only way to really experience inner calm is to turn inside and focus on one's own thoughts and feelings. Our perception of the reality that surrounds us may shift dramatically from one instant to the next. Additionally, our ideas, emotions, and feelings are in a state of perpetual flux. In spite of the fleeting nature of the experiences we have, we often get our sense of identity from the environment around us, which is also constantly changing.

Because the people, events, and circumstances in which we find ourselves have a continuous influence on our sense of identity, this sense of identity is in continual flux. When the world around us lives up to the standards we've set for it, we experience an increase in positive feelings about who we are. When our expectations aren't realized, we often feel a range of negative emotions, including anxiety, wrath, and disappointment. Anger, fear, and happiness are all examples of emotions. When we identify with our feelings, we transform ourselves into those feelings. When we allow ourselves to get identified with our ideas, we transform into those thoughts. Our ideas are what generate our perception of the world around us. If we allow our sense of identity to be determined by our fleeting experiences or if we continue to let our sense of self to be in a state of perpetual flux, then we will never be able to feel real inner peace.

It is a prevalent misconception that practicing meditation is synonymous with evading reality and that those who meditate are too focused on themselves. That couldn't be farther from the truth if you tried! We are able to rise beyond the illusions of reality that the vast majority of our species is mired in by regularly engaging in meditation practices, particularly those associated with Buddhism. When it comes to the idea that meditating is for those who are too focused on themselves, the fact is that we cannot show other people a different way to live our lives unless individuals first learn to experience the deeper truths that lie inside themselves. When a critical mass of such people is achieved, there will be a shift in the collective consciousness that is needed to stem the tide of our non-sustainable behaviors, actions that endanger the survival of life on earth. This change in the collective consciousness is required in order to put a stop to the tide of our non-sustainable behaviors.

Effective Advice On How To Meditate

In this chapter, you will discover many techniques that might help you improve your meditation practice. These recommendations may be of assistance to you at any time of day or night, regardless of where you are or what hour it is.

20 Suggestions to Calm Your Racing Thoughts

Many people believe that meditation is the practice of learning how to concentrate one hundred percent of one's attention on a single point. The practice is associated with several positive health effects, some of which include improved attention, enhanced emotions of happiness, and a reduction in feelings of worry. Even while many people experiment with meditation at some point in their life, only a tiny fraction of those people are able to maintain their practice for an amount of time that allows them to experience its positive effects. This is a really bad turn of events, and it's probable that this is why some people are reluctant to give it a go. Your frame of mind is the single most important factor.

1. Give the routine a more official air. Setting aside certain amounts of time each day for meditation is required in order to advance to the next level. I strongly recommend that you put forth some kind of effort at least twice every single day.

2. Start by focusing on your breathing. When you take long, steady breaths, your heart rate drops, which in turn relaxes your muscles and brings your attention to the present moment. It is a fantastic method for getting started with your practice.

3. Stretch your muscles before you get started. Your muscles and tendons will become more flexible once you stretch them. You will be able to sit or lay down

in a more relaxed position as a result. Stretching is great, but you need also pay attention to the rest of your body.

4. Make sure you have a goal in mind while you meditate. Meditation is a form of active process, and those just starting out need to be aware of this fact. This art form is challenging at first, and you will need to be actively involved in order to make progress.

5. You could start to feel frustrated. This is something that may often be noticed in novices. You can find yourself wondering why you are doing this or why it is so difficult for you to focus on what you are doing. This is a mental challenge that may be overcome with consistent effort and time spent practicing. You need to concentrate more.

6. Tune into your physical self. When you feel the beginnings of a meditative state taking hold of you, it is a good exercise for beginners to bring their

attention to their bodies. After the mind has become still, you should start paying attention to your feet and then gently move your way up the rest of your body. Be careful to mention the organs found within the body. This is a good sign, especially for someone starting off, since it shows that they are moving in the right direction.

7. Try out different positions in the game. The vast majority of people are under the mistaken impression that meditation entails sitting in a certain yoga position with one's legs crossed. You may practice meditation in any posture that is most comfortable for you, including laying down, sitting on a chair, or any other position.

8. Designate a specific space in which you will meditate. You will need to be certain that the room in question is not one in which you work, sleep, or engage in physical activity. Put some candles or other items related to your spiritual

practice in this space so that you may relax more easily.

9. Educate yourself on how to meditate. Participating will assist you in focusing more effectively and will help you have a deeper comprehension of this activity.

10. Resolve to follow through. Meditation is a way of life, and if you stop doing it, you will no longer get the benefits of it. It requires a lot of practice.

11. Relax your mind by listening to soothing music. You will find it easier to concentrate if you listen to music that is calming and serene but does not include voices. It is of assistance to you during the procedure.

12. Throughout the course of your day, give yourself opportunities to be mindful. It is a terrific technique to actually grow the meditation habit to find a breath or be present when you are not in your regular meditation area. You may do this by practicing mindfulness.

13. Ensure that there are no interruptions or diversions. The failure to establish peace is among the most common and serious errors that beginning students make. If you discover that you haven't switched off your phone or given the order to be silent, then you will not be able to locate the tranquil area that you need to be in for your meditation to truly be effective.

14. Take note of the minor alterations. For those just starting out with meditation, even the smallest motions have the potential to shift your experience from one of dissatisfaction to one of regeneration. These alterations are so subtle that an observer from the outside wouldn't even notice them, yet for the meditator, they may make all the difference in the world.

15. Make use of candlelight. Beginners can find it difficult to get used to meditating with their eyes closed at first. You may improve your ability to

concentrate by lighting one or more candles and using them as a focal point in your meditation or yoga practice. It has the potential to be quite effective.

16. Make sure you don't let yourself get worked up. This is the most vital piece of advice, yet it might be challenging for novices. Do not allow yourself to get stressed over the issue, no matter what occurs when you are attempting to meditate. This also involves having concerns about the practice of meditation.

17. Do it with a friend. We, as human beings, may sometimes get something by meditating in the company of other people or with a trusted companion. You may discuss the advantages of meditation with a close friend or member of your family and then meditate together. It is possible to transform it into a cooperative endeavor that will benefit both of you if you have someone who is cheering for you and you are rooting for that person as well.

18. Start your day with some morning meditation. The wee hours of the morning are just perfect for a set period of time to practice. There is less noise, and the regular junk that fills your head on a daily basis is absent. There is a lower possibility that you may get distracted as a result of this. Establishing a routine in which you rise at least a half an hour before the rest of the house in order to meditate is a healthy habit.

19. Always remember to be thankful for the experience. After you have finished meditating, take a few moments to reflect on the fact that you were given the chance to engage in this activity and that your mind was able to remain focused.

20. Take note if you find that your interest is starting to wane. Beginning a practice of meditation requires a lot of effort. There will come a time when it seems that it no longer fits into the "picture" that you have in your head.

Please take note of this fact. It is at this time that you will need to put in the most effort into your practice.

What Does It Mean To Meditate With A Guide?

One or more persons meditate while being led through the process by an experienced practitioner or instructor. This kind of meditation is referred to as guided meditation.

It is possible to lead a guided meditation session in person, or it may be done by written material, sound recording, video or other audiovisual media, music or vocal instruction, or even a mix of the two.

A guided meditation is one in which you can literally depend on additional assistance to focus your attention, as the name indicates. This kind of meditation goes by that term for a reason.

Those who have been honing their skills for a considerable amount of time may find it really easy to do. However, for those who are just beginning out, it may not seem to be that straightforward, but it is feasible.

Because we are used to thinking about many things at once, sustaining attention may seem challenging to those who are in the habit of doing so. This issue may be resolved via the practice of guided meditation.

What are the advantages of doing so?

In this book, you will learn about the many advantages of guided meditation. There are several advantages to be gained by making use of this resource to learn how to connect with both your body and your mind. Take a look at:

- Has a calming effect: The benefits of guided meditation include both mental and physical relaxation. In addition to this, it assists in the management of symptoms that are associated with stress.

-Makes it easier to relax: If you use guided meditation to help you relax, you'll find that the sensation of calm is more accessible and stays with you for longer.

-Improves the quality of your sleep: Techniques of guided sleep meditation may assist you in relaxing and taking control of your thoughts, which can often prevent one from falling or staying asleep. This has the potential to shorten the amount of time it takes to nod off and improve the overall quality of sleep.

-Helps in the treatment of depression: Feelings of discouragement, melancholy, and pessimism may be lessened with a better self-image and a more optimistic attitude on life, all of which are strengthened by mantras and the instructions given during guided meditation.

The practice of meditation entails the method of self-observation, which may be directed toward the act of breathing in and out or toward the thoughts and emotions that come up in response to an external stimulus.

In addition to promoting relaxation and acting as a potent instrument for personal development, scientific research continues to show that meditation may be an effective treatment for mood disorders such as depression and anxiety, as well as panic disorder.

CHAPTERS 4 AND 5

Your Body in Its Totality Our bodies, in their whole, are fairly extraordinary. Our bodies are humming with activity on the inside, and we are constantly moving because our internal systems are working like a well-oiled machine to keep us upright, breathing, and alive to see another day. As the blood travels via its vessels, the organs go about their business in relative silence. Oxygen is transported throughout the body, providing nourishment to our cells and ensuring that we remain alive.

However, we hardly never take the time to think about our bodies in their entirety.

When we have aches and pains, our attention is directed on them. My head, my toe, and my lower back are all killing me. Ouch. And it's those exact locations that feel fantastic while you're in the midst of moments of pleasure.

During my meditation sessions, I often get the sensation that I need something to help me feel more grounded and to redirect my attention back to my physical body. Something to briefly bring my attention back to the here and now, to my breathing and the stream of ideas that are flowing through my head.

Nothing is as helpful for me as concentrating on the whole of my body at the same time. A sudden realization of the contours of my sketch in their entirety. Trying to picture the shapes and lines of my body. Trying to picture a bright light emanating from my body and spreading out in all directions.

When you first begin to sense your edges, the border between where you end and the world starts, it is almost as if you can feel a shining or a pulse. the manner in which the air around you is making contact with those lines.

Bringing this awareness into your day may also serve as a highly effective strategy for practicing mindfulness. You can do it anywhere, but I prefer to try to make it a habit that I utilize when I'm in bed, both when I wake up in the morning and when I go to sleep at night. You can do it anywhere. When you are next lying in bed, give it a go by giving it a try.

Become aware of your body as it relaxes. a knowledge of your outline as well as how the exact edge of that shape interacts with its surroundings. The gentle pressure of the sheets under you and the refreshing breeze that blows from above. The gentleness of the cushion contrasts with the more pressing pressure that is placed on your heels. What each of your fingers is making contact with, whether it be air or an item. Every single one of those differences. A sensation that occurs at the edge of your skin as you breathe in or out.

You may also utilize this visualization technique when you're in a circumstance that makes you feel uncomfortable. When you first become aware of the sense of pain, take a time to shut your eyes, take a deep steady breath, and really focus on feeling the perimeter of your body as well as the way in which your body is supporting you. Do this for a few moments. You are safe and sound no matter what situations may be threatening, troubling, or facing you from the outside world. It might also be helpful to remind yourself that no matter what is being projected at you, you have the ability to choose to emanate love and kindness.

This is a really powerful method for centering yourself in your body and bringing awareness to thoughts that are wandering off topic or that are causing you to worry about an emotion or a circumstance. The attention that your mind is paying to the body brings you back to the here and now, to the place where you are really alive and breathing at this precise moment. And it is the one and only thing that is significant.

Your physical self is not there in the event that you are fixating on from the past, nor is it present in the event that you are anxiously anticipating in the future. It may be found right at this same now.

Please take a minute to become more aware of the contours of your body. The point at which either your feet or the seat underneath you contact the earth. The assistance provided by the surface upon which you are sitting or standing. Perform a full body scan; it won't take you more than a few seconds to finish. Now try to get a sense of what it's like to feel your whole body, including its weight, its lines, and its shapes.

Your physical being is always firmly rooted in the here and now. It offers an additional base, comparable to the fact that your breath is always there for you to return to with nothing more than a little moment of awareness.

Advice On Establishing A Routine For Daily Meditation

We are all aware that regular practice of meditation may be an excellent technique to manage stress and bring emotional equilibrium to our lives. Nevertheless, despite the vast number of advantages it offers, many practitioners still find it challenging to get into it. Now, the issue that has to be asked is, given that the stresses of day-to-day life tend to pull people down, how do you manage to do it regularly? Here are some suggestions on how you might urge yourself to make regular meditation a habit, in case you're seeking for some ideas to spark your imagination.

Devote a significant amount of time to meditating.

To begin, you will need to allot a sufficient amount of time each day for your meditation practice. Find a few minutes in the midst of your hectic schedule when you won't be interrupted so that you may collect your ideas and write them down. Some people do it in the morning before they get started on their job, while others do it in the evening before they call it a day and go to bed. Both times, though, are considered to be the most productive. Whatever kind of meditation you choose to practice, ensure that you give yourself the time to complete each session without feeling rushed. If you get the impression that you're being hurried through it, it might be challenging to truly get into it.

Consider the advantages that come from regular practice.

A powerful method for maintaining motivation is to regularly remind oneself of the positive outcomes that result from daily meditation. Why? Because having the consistent feeling that all of your hard work is for something worthwhile is helpful. Let's be honest: mediating isn't exactly the easiest thing in the world. It takes dedication, perseverance, and, of course, a self-disciplined and resolute desire to accomplish. If you concentrate on how challenging it is, you won't be motivated to really get it done. When you direct your attention on the outcomes, you not only increase the likelihood of really getting on with it, but you also get a feeling of success and relief after you've completed it. This is because focusing on the outcomes makes you more likely to actually get on with it.

Don't be overly critical of your own actions.

You should not expect to get the technique flawless the first time you try it, regardless of the method you use. Because effective meditation is analogous to a talent that must be developed, you should try not to be too severe on yourself if you discover that it involves some work on your part. Always try to keep your expectations in control because if you don't, you can end up feeling disappointed when whatever it is that you have been anticipating doesn't happen. Acquire the ability to take things one day at a time and learn to enjoy the journey as a whole. With consistent effort, you will begin to see improvements in your performance.

Download several applications for meditation.

Utilizing meditation applications may help you make the most of the benefits that technology has to offer. The good news is that there are a number of resources available for mobile that you can use to help you transform meditation into a regular habit. These tools include apps, websites, and audio recordings. When selecting a meditation software, you should make sure that it caters to both your own preferences and the way you live your life. You may also maintain a schedule of your meditation practice on your mobile device so that you can keep track of your sessions on a daily basis. This will allow you to feel more in control of your meditation routine.

Make the choice to meditate, and stick to it.

It is up to you and no one else to make a choice about this matter. If you don't feel it in your heart, don't let other people convince you that you should do it. If you give other people the authority to make decisions for you, you are giving that power to them, and it will be difficult for you to appreciate the things that you are doing for yourself. If you want to reap all of the advantages, you need to make this choice on your own and then stick to it. Because of this, if you want meditation to ultimately become your default behavior, you will need to engage in it in a way that is purposeful if you want it to become a habit.

There are a lot of folks who become anxious about whether or not they are meditating correctly. Try not to worry too much about your meditation practice; it will be some time before you get the hang of it, and in the meanwhile, just be patient. You won't have to wait long before you start enjoying the advantages of doing it frequently and making constant efforts to improve your technique as long as you find the time to accomplish both of those things.

The Dance Of Giving And Receiving That Occurs Between Children And Their Parents

It is often stated that there must be a balance of giving and receiving in relationships in order to keep the equilibrium and ensure that things go as smoothly as possible inside the connection. However, something like this is not allowed to occur between parents and their children. The gift of life has been bestowed to us by our parents, and for that we need to be grateful. However, there is no activity that can balance the act of giving life. As children, we will always be on the receiving end of our parents' generosity because of the nature of our relationship. This is the way in which each one of us contributes to the service of life. Even our parents had to start out as children, and it was their parents who gave them the gift of life. However, they are not capable of matching that action. When we have children of our own, we will be in a position similar to that of the giver, and we will provide more for them. However, our offspring are unable to return us. It makes the lives of children more difficult when they strive to strike a balance between giving and getting from their parents. Even if the parents choose to take more from their children, this will still cause disruptions in the flow of life and love that is contained inside the system.

If a kid continually feels that they need to offer more to their parents than they have given him or her, then the connection between parents and children has become unbalanced.

- As things are, a youngster is not receptive to accepting further support from his parents.

- The kid should give the parents more, while the parents want to get more from the child.

Parents have given their children this life without passing any judgements on it; rather, they have provided life in its "as it is" form. It is now the responsibility of the children to accept this life in its "as it is" form. There are times when children feel that the life they have been given is a burden, or they feel the need to provide more to their parents so that they may repay the favor. Both of these feelings are common. However, one must comprehend the fundamental idea behind life, which states that providing a living environment for children is not a favor done by parents. They have been of use to life. And now it is time for the kid to conduct the first service toward life, which is to receive life with respect, honor, appreciation, and grace. This is the first step in the child's journey toward becoming a mature adult. Absolutely nothing can be altered or changed about it in any way.

When a kid makes an effort to cut a parent out of their life by providing justifications such as the parent's failure to live up to certain standards or the child's perception that the parent hasn't done a good job of meeting their obligations, the child will eventually begin to experience a hollow sensation on the inside. There is something lacking and unfinished about them. One cannot reach their full potential until they have reconciled their relationship with both of their parents and come to terms with the life they have been given.

There may be moments when our parents will harm us, but we have to allow that pain to have a home in our hearts as well. Obviously, it is not feasible to instantaneously free oneself from the mental anguish that accompanies the physical agony. In addition, there is no need for us to put undue stress on ourselves in order to become a perfect saint. At that time, it is necessary for you to address the hurt, the anguish, and the emotions and sentiments that are occurring on the inside of you. Everything that can be traced back to them must be accepted in its current form. If a child can learn to accept their parents without trying to change who they are or how they were raised, they will see a significant improvement in the overall quality of their life. We should refrain from condemning them since it's possible that this is the kind of upbringing they had from their parents when they were younger. When one is feeling upset, they should just envision the parent who has caused them pain and say to yourself, "I understand the hurt that is within you, and I also understand the hurt that you have given me." The pain that you've caused me, I let it take up residence in my heart just as it is. I accept the blessings you have bestowed upon me in this life, and I resolve to use them for the betterment of myself and others.

When you say this, you are immediately embracing life as it is, and with the good that is already in you, you are ready to start creating an experience that is filled with even more happiness and success.

When we are willing to let go of the illusions that we allow ourselves to believe on a day-to-day basis and instead open ourselves up to the greater truth that exists in life, we discover that we are able to experience more inner peace. The ability to notice both the good and the bad aspects of a situation gets simpler. Recognizing something or someone gives you the strength to accept them or their circumstances as they are. There is no place for any type of criticism or fear in this space. The act of acknowledgment gives you an inner sense of power, enables you to make more educated decisions in life, and broadens your perspective on the value of the knowledge you've gained.

Techniques Of Meditation That Are Simple To Perform

Open-ended and closed-ended practices are the two primary classifications that may be used to organize all varieties of contemplative practices. Open-ended practice is a kind of meditation in which you do not concentrate on any one item in particular but instead allow your mind to wander freely and pay attention to anything catches your attention. During a drill with a closed door, you choose an item of concentration and then concentrate your attention on that thing. In this chapter, we will provide you with one exercise that has a closed end and two that have an open end.

There are literally hundreds of different meditation techniques available, but I've found that the simplest ones are the most helpful when I'm just starting out.

Being mindful Meditation Based on Breathing

You can unleash awareness by relaxing, unwinding, and opening up your body and mind with this really simple meditation practice. This is a contemplative exercise with little opportunities for expansion. Work on the following to have some experience with it:

After you have finished working on the seven aspects of posture, you should set a timer for five minutes.

Because your breath serves as the object of concentration in this exercise, you will need to direct all of your attention to it.

Take a breath in via your nose, and while you do so, bring your attention to the ways in which the air moving into and around your body causes movement there.

Exhale through your nostrils, and while you do so, bring your attention to the process of how exhalation causes air to leave your body.

Maintain your focus on your breath and make an effort to merge with it.

It is possible that your mind may start to wander throughout the exercise; if this occurs, gently draw your focus back to your breath and reassure yourself that you will take care of all of your other issues once the session is over.

You just need to do it a few times, and after a week of constant practice, you should be able to concentrate more on your breathing.

Be careful not to give up on the exercise, and make it a habit to do it every day, even if just for five minutes. Increase the time spent on it gradually until you reach ten, fifteen, and ultimately twenty minutes. After some time has passed, you will notice that you are able to focus better on every work that you do and that you are able to thoroughly and quietly experience each moment.

Meditation For Kids, Both Beginners And Busy Kids'

The fact that the children of my friends meditate on their own, without being instructed to do so, astounds and inspires me. I have inquired as to what prompted them to begin meditating as well as the length of time that they devote to this practice on a regular basis. As a result of their responses, I made the decision to include a straightforward meditation that was developed especially for young people.

Our children and grandchildren are being subjected to a sensory overload in today's environment, which is having a negative effect on both their physical health and their level of happiness.

Children as young as three are starting to watch television, developing an addiction to the time they spend in front of screens, and getting overstimulated and overloaded with information from other channels than those dedicated to cartoons and programming designed specifically for children.

kids grow anxious and afraid when kids watch and listen to newscasts or overhear adult discussions that transmit the atrocities that are taking place throughout the globe. It is possible for them to have symptoms such as an inability to sleep, teeth grinding, stomach problems, and even depression. In addition to everything else, youngsters tend to get busy. occupied with studies as well as extracurricular activities after school. They are just as busy as their parents.

The following is a suggestion for parents who are really busy: why don't you take some time out of your hectic schedule to meditate along with your kid? This will not only help them become more self-assured and achieve mastery over their feelings, but it will also assist in the development of a unique connection between the two of you.

You have the ability to provide your kid with the skills that will assist them in ridding themselves of stressful, negative thoughts and emotions while simultaneously fostering the development of self-confidence and empathy in them. This is a fun exercise that the whole family can participate in together, either one-on-one or as a group.

This is an introduction to a brief visualization meditation that is suitable for beginners and children who are always on the go. The use of the balloon as an illustration for a breathing technique is something that I really love doing with younger children. It is also appropriate for children older than 10 years old to utilize. I find that I even use it for myself sometimes!

You may find it helpful to take the role of storyteller and lead them through this meditation the first few times they try it, or at least until they feel comfortable doing it on their own.

How to go about it

1. Find a spot to sit that is comfortable, peaceful, and secure.

2. Place your hands in such a way that they are comfortable on your lap.

3. While you are closing your eyes, think of anything that has made you feel sad, angry, or unhappy in the recent past or now.

4. Picture yourself holding a deflated balloon in the fourth position. Imagine the hue, the contours, and the proportions of it. You are the only one who has this balloon.

5. Take a long, deep breath in through your nose, and then exhale all of your bad emotions by blowing them into the balloon via your mouth.

6. Take a few long, slow breaths in. Take a deep breath and fill your heart with loving and joyful thoughts.

7. Expel once again, this time from the lower part of your stomach, all of those unwelcome emotions.

8. Visualize and imagine the balloon becoming larger while it is in your hands.

9. Continue to repeat the activities of breathing in feelings of love and happiness and breathing out feelings of sorrow, anger, or negativity until all of these emotions have left your body. This may be done by repeating the steps until all of these emotions have left your body.

10. Once the balloon has reached its capacity, you should release it. Imagine that the balloon is rising further and higher into the air, carrying all of those negative emotions away with it as it goes.

11. Now breathe in compassion and kindness, allowing yourself to feel at ease and at peace.

12. Give yourself a bear hug and express gratitude to yourself.

The Importance Of Modesty In Meditation

The aforementioned passage from "The Prophet" has the Khalil Gibran statement that I like the most, maybe out of all of his other works. This was the quote that illuminated for me just what it was that I had been going about my life all wrong. My life had much too much chaos. There was no opportunity for people to be quiet. Meditation gives you the opportunity to experience stillness, yet this silence has the potential to reveal a great deal about who you are. In order to exemplify my point, I need you to think of a location that is easily accessible from your house and that makes you feel utterly amazed. For me, it was a mountaintop that offered a sweeping view over the surrounding agricultural landscape. At the top of that hill, there was a little church, and it was when I was seated on a stone in front of that church that I first understood the meaning of the lines written by Khalil Gibran. In the stillness of the evening, as the sun was dipping below the horizon, I had an overwhelming sense of how little I was in the grand scheme of things. How exactly did it benefit me? Now, when you finally realize yourself for what you really are, you will start to rise up the ladder of comprehension. When you accept humility as a virtue, you unlock the ability to experience pleasure via movement. I was able to take in the beauty of the planet from that vantage point on top of that hill. It left me in amazement. It opened my eyes to how insignificant I was, but yet how important my role was in the whole situation. You have to realize that every single stone on a beach has a certain function. Every single grain of sand contributes to the stability of the other grains. There is a lesson to be learned from each every leaf that a tree loses. As a result, it followed that even though I was on the smaller side, I was nonetheless significant.

When you finally admit that you are human and capable of making mistakes, you open yourself up to a world of happiness. You also come to the realization that you have a role to perform in the world, which helps you put all of the things that are bothering you in their proper perspective. At that very moment, I was completely incapable of harboring any hostility. I experienced absolutely no negativity in any way, shape, or form, and sometimes you need to be alone with your thoughts in order to get perspective and listen to the voice inside your mind that tells you that you are an important part of this world and that this planet is an important part of you. When you stand at a position such as this, or even sit down as I did, you embrace humility, which is something that many people in today's society seem to have abandoned. When you see humility in action, it boggles your mind. There are a lot of posts on my Facebook page that are packed with quotes that imply that being humble might make you a better person. I see a lot of these posts. People read them, agree with them, and then go on to sharing photographs of their pets on social media, despite the fact that they don't really understand how such things can fit into their life. That that day, on that hill, I saw it, and if you want meditation to be effective for you, you need to do the same thing I did.

We put a lot of effort into conforming to expectations that have absolutely no bearing on who we are or how our lives are going to turn out. It is important to remove the distractions of possessions, material things, and the opinions of others if you want to be able to see who you truly are. If you can, it is beneficial to go somewhere in nature where you are surrounded by the beauty of the natural world and you are unable to ignore it. This will help you feel more humble, which is the first step toward practicing effective meditation. You don't anticipate anything, despite the fact that everything you need is there in front of you. It is provided for you by nature, so you do not need to demonstrate anything about who you are or what you believe in order to get it. I mean, that's really incredible, isn't it?

Sessions of yoga are often conducted in locations that are surrounded by natural scenery for the precise reason stated above. It's possible that the instructor picked the location because it was convenient for her, but having the class in a setting that is both beautiful and uplifting is much more beneficial. For example, in the sun salutation, a student begins in a rolled-up position and then gradually reaches up toward the sky, standing up on tiptoes to embrace nature and the day that is to come after it.

When you have a sense of humility, you get the following benefits, all of which are beneficial to your meditation practice:

You watch and take note of what's going on, but you don't pass judgment on it. You listen to what's being said, but you don't pass judgment on what's being said. You watch and take note of what's going on right now. This moment is the only one that exists. Yesterday is over, and tomorrow has not yet arrived. This now is all that counts.

It is easy to understand how something like this may be helpful during meditation. If you go into your bedroom with the intention of meditating, but your mind is already preoccupied with passing judgment on other people, you will find it difficult to focus on your breathing because unfavorable ideas about the other person will keep popping into your head. If you have a bad history, but you let it control your "now," then you are making your "now" just as awful as your history was. Consequently, letting go of thoughts about the past and focussing instead on the here and now will make you a lot happier and better able to focus on your meditation practice. Your thoughts are considered to be abstract if they are focused on something that is still in the future, such as a test or an interview that will take place tomorrow. Since that occurrence has not taken place as of yet, it is without importance at this moment.

You are able to overcome the difficulties that stand in the way of you being able to fight fear, hatred, envy, and all of the other bad components that you are letting into your life by approaching things with humility in your approach. You will be able to completely focus on your meditation practice if you follow the modest attitude and conceive of the here and now as a problem that is distinct from both the past and the future.

The practice of meditation is one that has been around for many thousands of years. This is because people who choose to practice it get new insights as a result of their participation. You won't fully understand why meditating has been practiced for such a long time and why so many people do it unless you try it for some length of time and stick with it. The following is a list of some of the advantages that have been confirmed by scientific research to be associated with meditation. This list is not meant to be comprehensive. Because meditation is a treatment for mental illness, and a great number of diseases can be traced back, either directly or indirectly, to involuntary thought processes, meditation is a treatment for mental illness. You will feel more at ease after meditating, and as a result, you could even give some thought to modifying some of your behaviors to lead a healthy lifestyle.

The many advantages of meditation have been the subject of a substantial number of research investigations in recent years. Again, the advantages may be broken down into their three primary subcategories: mental well-being, emotional well-being, and physical well-being. The following has been shown by tens of thousands of studies of a very high quality including a wide range of subjects and historical periods.

Meditation has the potential to reduce feelings of stress, anxiety, and impulsivity, all of which are detrimental to one's mental health. It fosters a healthy sense of self-esteem as well as self-acceptance. It not only helps people become more resilient against pain, but it also helps them become more relaxed, attentive, and optimistic. It has been shown to be beneficial in the development of healthy social relationships, as well as in the improvement of emotional intelligence, and in the prevention of emotional smoking and eating. In terms of enhancements to one's mental ability, it is helpful to learn how to control ADHD, to ignore distractions, and to absorb information in a more effective manner. It improves concentration and creativity, in addition to mental power and the ability to solve problems. It has a beneficial effect on the body's immunological system as well as the control of energy levels. It lowers blood pressure, lowers the risk of HIV as well as fibromyalgia and arthritis, and it improves lifespan (yes, it really lengthen life). It has also been shown to reduce the risk of heart and brain problems.

To put it another way, meditating has been shown to have a variety of positive effects, many of which have been proven by scientific research. To not practice meditation on a daily basis would indicate that you are as sane as a monkey. The arguments that one lacks the necessary resources, such as time or energy, to meditate are not valid. Because if you practiced meditation frequently, you'd have more time and energy for other things. Meditation has been shown to improve cognitive function as well as extend life expectancy. Therefore, it ought to improve both your lifespan and your ability to bring in monetary gain. If you consider it from this angle, you'll see that meditating will provide you with more time, money, and vitality. It does not cost anything, and the only thing that is required of you is a commitment to doing it for a specific amount of time in order to see significant improvements in your health.

The Brain Of An Active Elderly Person

Increased intellectual flexibility is yet another advantage that may be accrued via regular meditation practice. Some people find that becoming older brings with it an increased burden of ideas, feelings, and views, as well as an inability to flow with the difficulties and constraints that come with the stages of life. This may be a source of stress, and it is possible that it might even cause sickness. Because the majority of meditation practices place an emphasis on cultivating an awareness of one's thoughts, feelings, and physical sensations rather than cultivating an awareness of one's judgments about any experience, practicing mindfulness meditation may also assist in reducing one's attachment to predetermined outcomes, increasing one's mental flexibility, and adding to one's neural reserve.

Even while the findings are promising, it is essential to keep in mind that this study is still in its early stages, and the results have been inconsistent thus far. For instance, a number of studies have revealed that older meditators perform better than age-matched non-meditators, or operate in a manner that is comparable to that of younger participants on a range of interest tasks. Others have shown either little or no change in cognitive performance as a result of older persons participating in a mindfulness intervention, or they have reported that the benefits made are no longer sustained over time.

What we do know is that participating in mindfulness meditation for a significant amount of time over a period of time may also improve cognitive function in older individuals, and that these effects may also be maintained with continued practice of the technique. This is wonderful information for the tens of millions of people who are fighting against the devastating effects that becoming older has on the brain.

The Fundamentals of Practicing Mindfulness

Through practicing mindfulness, we are able to create some distance between ourselves and our responses, so dismantling our habitual reactions. The following is a guide that will help you tune into mindfulness at some point during the day:

Always be sure to schedule some downtime. This is due to the fact that in order to have access to your mindfulness abilities, you do not need a meditation cushion or bench, or any other sort of remarkable instruments; nonetheless, you will need to set aside some time and space for the practice.

Be mindful of the here and now in its unaltered state. The goal of practicing mindfulness is not, as it formerly was, to achieve mental stillness or to strive for a state of permanent calm. The goal is straightforward: rather than focusing on judgment, we want to pay attention to what is happening in the here and now. We are aware that this is easier to say than to accomplish.

Allow your opinions and assessments to pass. When we become aware that judgements are arising throughout the course of our practice, we have the ability to make a mental note of them and then allow them to pass.

Bring your focus back to gaze at the present second in its unaltered state. Our thoughts have a tendency to wander off in contemplation rather regularly. Because of this, the practice of mindfulness consists of bringing one's attention back to the here and now on a regular basis.

Give structure to your thoughts that is always roaming. Don't criticize yourself for the things that come to mind; rather, practice noticing when your train of thought has strayed and bringing it back in a non-threatening way.

This is the standard procedure. It's been mentioned a lot of times that it's quite straightforward, but it's not always easy to do what has to be done. The task consists mostly of continuing to do it.

The end result will make both the issue and itself far worse.

How you could address the matter most effectively via meditation

The practice that is known as meditation places an emphasis on the breath, not because there is something particularly unique about breathing, but rather because the physiological feeling of respiration is present at all times, and you may use it as an anchor to bring your attention back to the here and now. During the course of the practice, you may also find that you get preoccupied with ideas, feelings, or noises; regardless of where your attention wanders, bring it back to the present now by focusing on the next breath. It is not necessary for you to come back more than once; that is OK.

A Straightforward Method of Meditation

Relax and take a seat. Find a position that provides you with a seat that is secure, solid, and comfy all at the same time.

Take note of the movement that your legs are making. If you are sitting on a cushion, you should be able to easily move your legs in front of you. The following is one approach that may be taken: If you are sitting in a chair, place the soles of your feet on the ground.

You should attempt to straighten the upper portion of your body, but you shouldn't become rigid. Your back has a curve to it that is very normal. Just leave it in that there.

Take note of the motions your fingers are making. Place your palms in a position that is parallel to your upper body. Put the palms of your hands on your knees in whichever position seems most comfortable to you and rest your arms there.

Be careful to relax the intensity of your stare. You may do this by lowering your chin just a little and allowing your eyes to gradually go downward. There is no need that you must close your eyes. You don't need to pay attention to anything that seems to be in front of your eyes since you may just let it be.

Make sure you are aware of how you are breathing. Also, focus your attention on the feeling that occurs in your body when you breathe, whether that be the air passing through your mouth or nostrils, or the movement of your chest, belly, or both.

Take note of when your thoughts divert your attention away from your breathing. Your focus will go to other things in the room at some point, it's inevitable. Don't be concerned. There is no need to suppress or eliminate thought in any way. If you find that your thoughts are wandering, gently bring your focus back to your breathing.

Think about other things while your mind wanders. Additionally, you could discover that your thoughts are always straying; this is very natural. Rather of engaging in a battle with your thoughts, practice monitoring them instead of responding to them. Please take a seat and focus your attention. That's all there is, despite how difficult it is to keep up with and manage. Repeatedly and incessantly bring your attention back to your breath, excluding judgment and anticipation.

When you are ready, softly move your attention in the direction of the person who is speaking (if your eyes are closed, open them). Take a moment to listen carefully to the surrounding area and make note of any noises you hear. Take note of how your physical self feels exactly at this moment. Take note of your thoughts and feelings.

The Beginnings Of A Meditation Practice

Do not rush into meditation just yet without first ensuring the following things have been taken care of:

You are responsible for cultivating an appropriate setting.

The location would be determined by two factors: the amount of room that is available and the sort of lifestyle that you lead. You should make sure that the location you choose for your meditation practice is serene, comfortable, and filled with natural light. You don't even need to have a really complex environment. Just remember to make things as brief and basic as possible. Keep in mind that you are going to create your very own tranquil enclave in which to practice meditation. Do not give up if you are turned off by some noise from the outside that is not within your control, even if it is a significant amount of noise. With enough practice, you'll be able to put yourself into a meditative state regardless of where you are.

Find yourself a spot where you can relax.

After you have found a place that is quiet and peaceful, the next thing you need to do is search for a seat that is comfortable. It is recommended that if you are going to sit on a chair, you go for one that has a firm back support. Armchairs are off limits since they have a propensity to make you feel comfortable and cause you to nod off. If you're going to sit on the floor, you may as well bring a mat or a towel with you. You may also find additional comfort by using a pillow. You may want to consider covering yourself in a cozy blanket if you are going to be seated for a significant amount of time.

Meditation is going to be tough for you if you are in an uncomfortable posture, and even the slightest noise is going to be enough to pull your attention away from it. In addition to this, you will have a difficult time remaining seated for extended periods of time.

One session of meditation lasting five minutes is more than sufficient for a beginning.

It is recommended that those who are just starting out meditate for at least five minutes at a time. Especially if you are just starting out with meditation, engaging in this activity for an extended amount of time will not be useful. When compared to longer, less frequent sessions, shorter, more frequent ones are preferable. After some period of time, you can find that you are able to endure longer sessions and come up with a routine that works for you.

Unwinding is an important part of getting ready.

Before you start meditating, it is regarded a good ability to learn how to relax. This will help ensure that each meditation session is successful. The first thing you need to do is find a comfortable sitting position, which may be on the floor or on a chair. Take long, slow, and deliberate breaths. Feel your muscles relaxing while you repeat positive statements to yourself, such as "My muscles are relaxed," "My hands and arms are relaxing," "My mind is calm," "My body is calm," and "My mind is awake." Keep in mind that a calm state of mind and body may be quite beneficial to your health. It is simple to recognize a calm condition in a person by observing his body language.

Identify the Stress in Your Body

In conjunction with being calm, it is also essential that you detect any physical stresses, the majority of which may be located in the back, shoulders, and neck. These regions of the body often carry the whole of an individual's emotional stress. If you give the relaxation exercises a try, you could discover parts of your body that tend to remain tight and stressed out. You might try massaging those regions, but be careful not to put too much tension on any of the muscles.

Try joining both hands behind your head, bringing your shoulders back, and pressing your head into your hands to relieve stress in your neck. Put as much force as you can muster into both hands. Should there be anxiety that runs deep inside you, it may be time to examine the way you live your life. Are you more of a slob or an athlete? Do you often go to bed without even getting in a workout? It is important to keep in mind that releasing any areas of physical tension before beginning meditation can help you sit more comfortably.

Take breaths from deep into your diaphragm.

There are a lot of individuals who hardly pay attention to how they breathe. This is one of the most essential lessons you may acquire before beginning your meditation practice. Put one hand on your upper chest and breathe normally while doing so. Become aware of the rise and fall of your chest as you breathe. When you meditate, you will become aware that you are breathing consciously. You will pay close attention to the rhythmic cycle of your breath as well as the rising and falling movement of your lungs, belly, and diaphragm as you inhale and exhale.

When you breathe in, be sure to take lengthy, deep breaths via your nose until the air reaches your abdomen, at which point it will have passed through your diaphragm. When you exhale, the opposite of what you just did should happen. Be conscious of the little pause that occurs between each inhalation and exhalation, and feel each breath move through your abdominal region.

The significance of counting one's breaths

This is a typical exercise that brings the mind and the body into harmony with one another. When counting your breaths, you should do your best not to let yourself get distracted or lose track of the number of breaths you have counted in your head. In the practice of meditation, this is also a helpful technique. Mentally counting from one to 10 is a good place to start. Once you feel comfortable with it, you should attempt counting as you inhale. That would make one for the total. The number two is assigned to the moment when you exhale. Exercice this method of counting until it becomes second nature to you.

Counting your breaths is often recommended as a kind of preliminary preparation for meditation since it helps your mind become more focused.

What You Need To Know Before Engaging In Imaginative Meditation

Creative meditation may be practiced at any time and in any location, but it is most helpful when you have a certain spot that you use to meditate in, such as a favorite chair or a section of a room that is exclusively yours.

Before you begin your creative meditation, there are a few things you should think about, including the following:

Do not convince yourself that you are too busy to engage in creative meditation; in reality, it need not take very much time at all. It may last as little as a minute or two, or it could go on for an hour or even longer. You are able to make it work for you and adapt it to your way of life. You don't need a specific room or space in your house to meditate, especially when you're just getting started. However, if you want to, you may practice this ancient practice anywhere: on a train, in the park, at your workplace, etc.

When you have just finished a substantial meal, it might be difficult to meditate since your body needs time and energy to digest the food. It can be difficult to find a comfortable sitting position and maintain concentration after eating.

Consider having a bath, a shower, or engaging in any other activity that will help you unwind and get into a more optimistic frame of mind before you start the task at hand, if you have the opportunity to do so. since of this, the advantages of meditation may be enhanced since you will already be in a calm state when you sit down to meditate.

Find a place in your home where there is peace and quiet and where you won't be bothered so that you may meditate creatively if at all possible. To foster a feeling of tranquility in the space, light a candle or burn some incense before you enter. Make sure the space is nice and toasty, and the lighting isn't too harsh.

Make sure that you are comfortable by wearing loose clothing that is pleasant to sit in and that will keep you warm while you are sitting motionless.

Before you begin your creative meditation, give giving calm, deep breathing a try. Relax as you let each breath out at its own natural rate, and notice how you are gradually getting more at peace.

You should meditate at a time that is convenient for you. It's best to do it first thing in the morning or just before you go to bed at night, but do it whenever it fits into your life the best. A feeling of regularity may be created by meditating at the same time and location on a regular basis, which can also assist you in maintaining momentum.

Before you sit down to do your creative meditation, it may be beneficial to walk about a little bit to enhance your circulation and release some of the stress that has built up in your body. Stretch out your arms and legs while standing with your feet planted firmly on the ground and your legs and hips slightly apart. Move your arms from side to side while you do this. Move in a way that is natural for your body.

When seated, you have the option of sitting on a chair or a cushion placed on the floor; choose whatever option is most comfortable for you. When you are sitting on a chair, attempt to position yourself so that your spine is in a straight line by sitting on the edge of the chair. The slightest forward tilt of the hips might provide additional support for the back.

While you are engaged in your creative meditation, maintain a pleasant grin on your face. Maintaining a calm and relaxed state is made easier with a pleasant grin.

If at first you find that your mind is unable to focus, give yourself a break.

It's possible that you may get quickly annoyed, but you need to work as hard as you can to keep that from happening. The more you do it, the simpler it will become. When you become aware that your mind is wandering, give yourself a kind smile and try to bring your focus back.

After you have finished your creative meditation, remain seated for a little longer so that you may savor the feeling of serenity and quiet. Make an effort to carry these emotions with you as you go about the rest of your day.

www.ingramcontent.com/pod-product-compliance
Lightning Source LLC
Chambersburg PA
CBHW050243120526
44590CB00016B/2195